12 Past Midnight

A Journey Into The Shadow

Josef Desade
Illustrated by Gareth Walsh

Special thanks to

Gareth Walsh
Christine Wozkniak
Sapphire Luna Rios
Cliff Poulin

For Howard Atkins

*"I think there are a set of experiences
that turn a potential writer into a
working writer, and then there
are places in your life where you
start to recognize what you want to do."*
-Stephen King

"Who looks outside, dreams;
who looks inside, awakes."
-C.G. Jung

A warm summer breeze wafts the scent of cloves...as the sky becomes a place that no light knows...contemplation marks this night...meditation; third sight...underneath the insects and evening sounds...serenity in Sahasrara is found...where wisdom abounds amongst the petals...within the Earth where decomposed everything settles...the crescent watches, a silent witness...to the beauty of the never ending cycle of life and death's kisses...round full circle everything goes...following the astral ebbs and flows.

Echoing, resounding...open the door...a pornographic snuff film of absolutely no consequence...dreams filter in and out and the subconscious carries on it's march...the rain falls outside...everything else is quiet, as if the world was washed away...and there is nothing but the rain and thee...the rain and thee.

©Gareth Walsh 2014

Stillness...no sound except the solitary drip from age old trees...a mist settles across the land...blotting out the houses in it's haze...serenity is found where humanity has vanished...tranquil moments are only discovered after the incessant noise ceases and I find myself alone...no sound of voices...no metallic pollution ringing threw the air...no shouts and confusion...just the finality of silence and the sounds of the earth.

As darkness descends I watch the shadows creep...parasitic leeches begging for a taste of my soul...the past is a forgotten tale...a fable that fades into the mists of time...always seeming further away...the present is but a ticking clock...everything is at a standstill...I hear the passing seconds yet the future is yet to be determined...absolution is yet to be reached for the sins of the past and the karmic wheel turns on...vampires claw at every door...begging to have just a taste...begging for a glimpse of the psyche...a taste of within...leaving me a dried husk...a shell...forgotten with the past...yet the clock ticks on.

Under starlit skies the stillness is deafening...everything motionless...transitory shutter images...flicker...flicker...the puppet show rests under a crescent moon...laughter from above; a farce...an eternal comedy as the clouds consume, extinguished in a wisp of smoke.

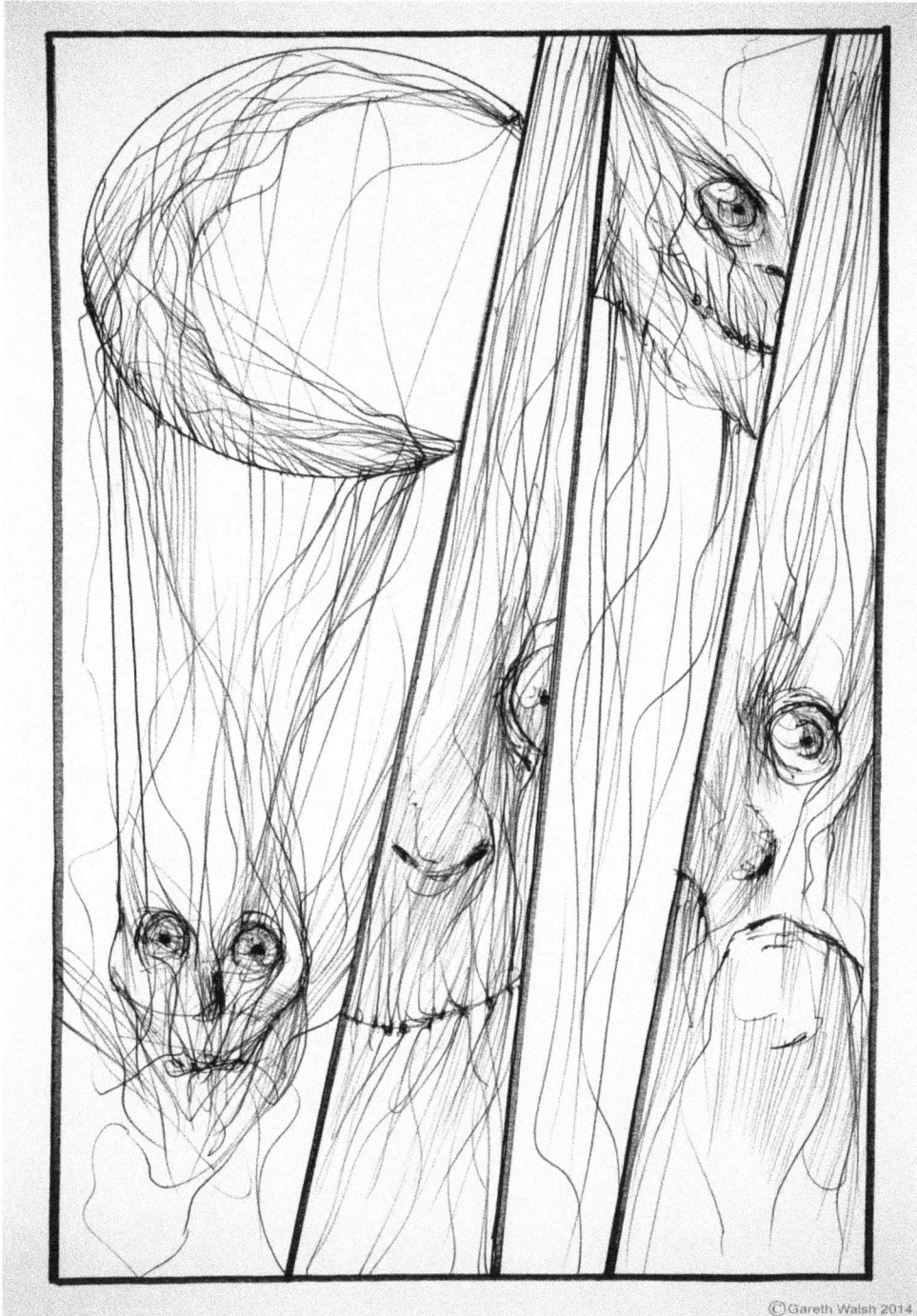

The church bell tower rang...resounding across the land...a cold freeze covered the Earth and the sheep traveled from near and far...herding towards a false prophet...spreading like a disease to blemish the face of every corner of the globe...and when the slaughter came...all were silent.

©Gareth Walsh 2014

And as if in a midsummer dream, the smoke curled in tendrils around my fingers...a contemplative breeze carried the scent of lilies and for a moment I found peace...perfect serenity...I gazed upon the slowly descending sun and breathed in the air...nightfall neared.

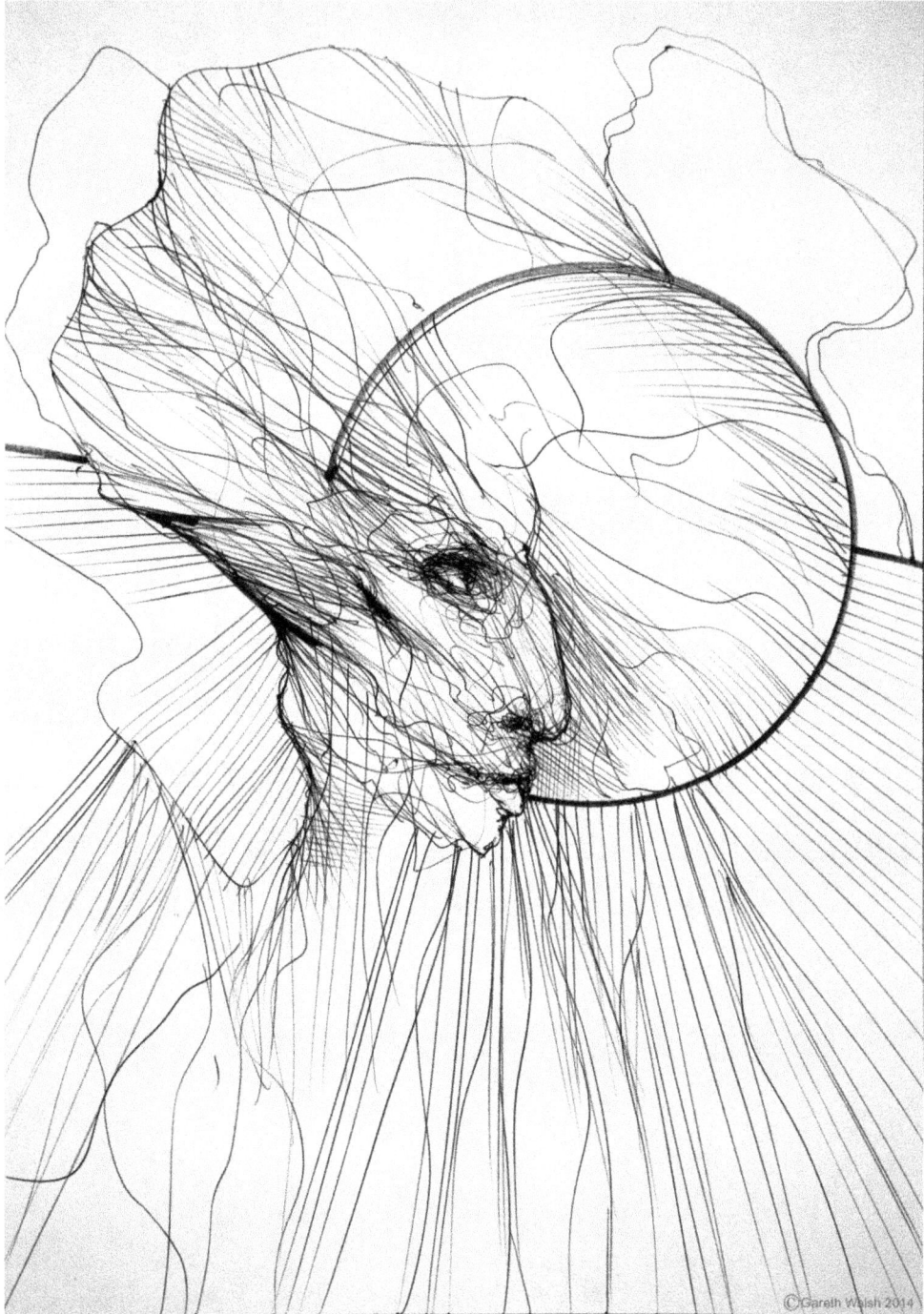

© Gareth Walsh 2014

A portrait of misery...self inflicted remorse or deceitful guile...apathy; one true love...the empathy has long ago been turned out by the laughter from above...the moon looks down and laughs...fateful joke...divine retribution...the martyr wept tears of joy as the fool hung by his foot...the star glittered in the distance as the hierophant let out a cackle.

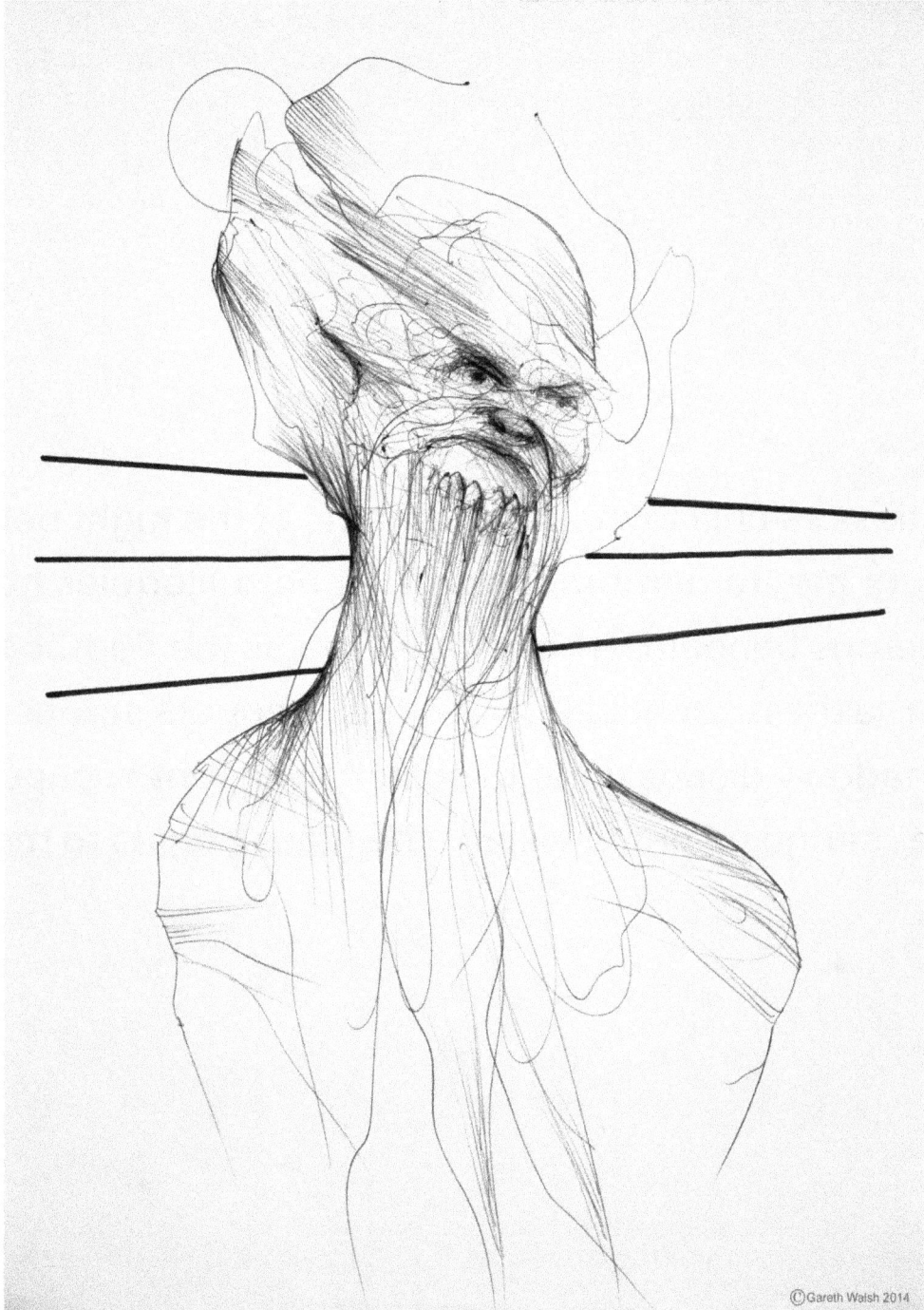

Restless...a chill to the skin...dreams of the night before haunt me...remembrances of cryptic soliloquies from skeletons beneath the bed taunt me as the floorboards groan...ashes...scent of burning flesh...fingers scrape from shadowy dispositions...a solitary moment escapes me...sanguine tinted vision...the glass begins to melt.

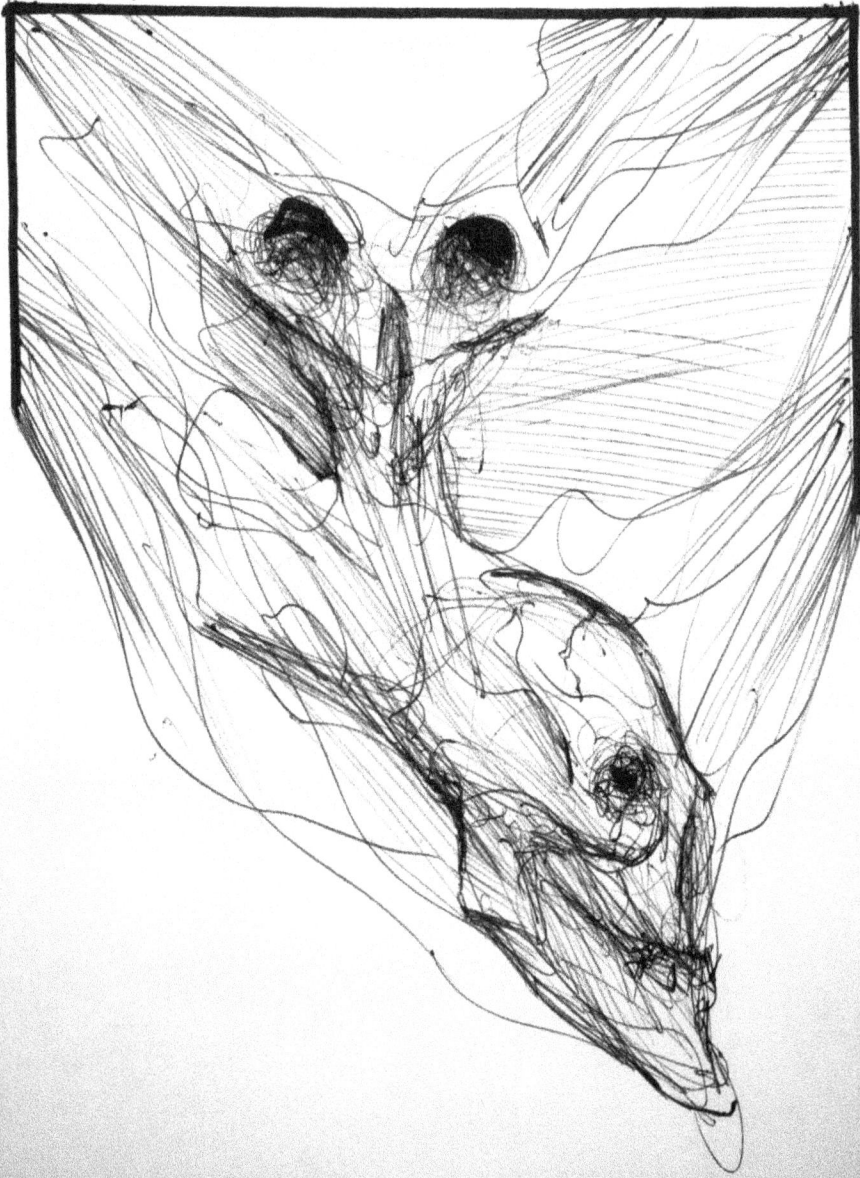

©Gareth Walsh 2014

Multifaceted reflections...a riddle within...a solitary sermon unfolds...crickets and cicadas argue relentlessly among the eavesdropping creatures of the night...a scream resonates into the cool night air...a question of faith...a god prays ferverently to a forgotten people...hope is lost...another name scrawled in the ledger of apostasy...Emmanuel.

EMMANUEL

© Gareth Walsh 2014

Androgynous faces peer from the shadows in the hall...footfalls...slowly, carefully creep...the scent of sulphur in the air...all an illusion...go back to sleep...beneath the boards...the furnace burns...a darkened veil is lifted...third sight...cloven feet...all an illusion...go back to sleep.

A question of morals...deceitful smiles and an air of arrogance...the scribe starves while the wicked grow fat...honor, a dead scene...sunlight plays shadows through broken glass...the dust settles...the curtain silently falls...end scene.

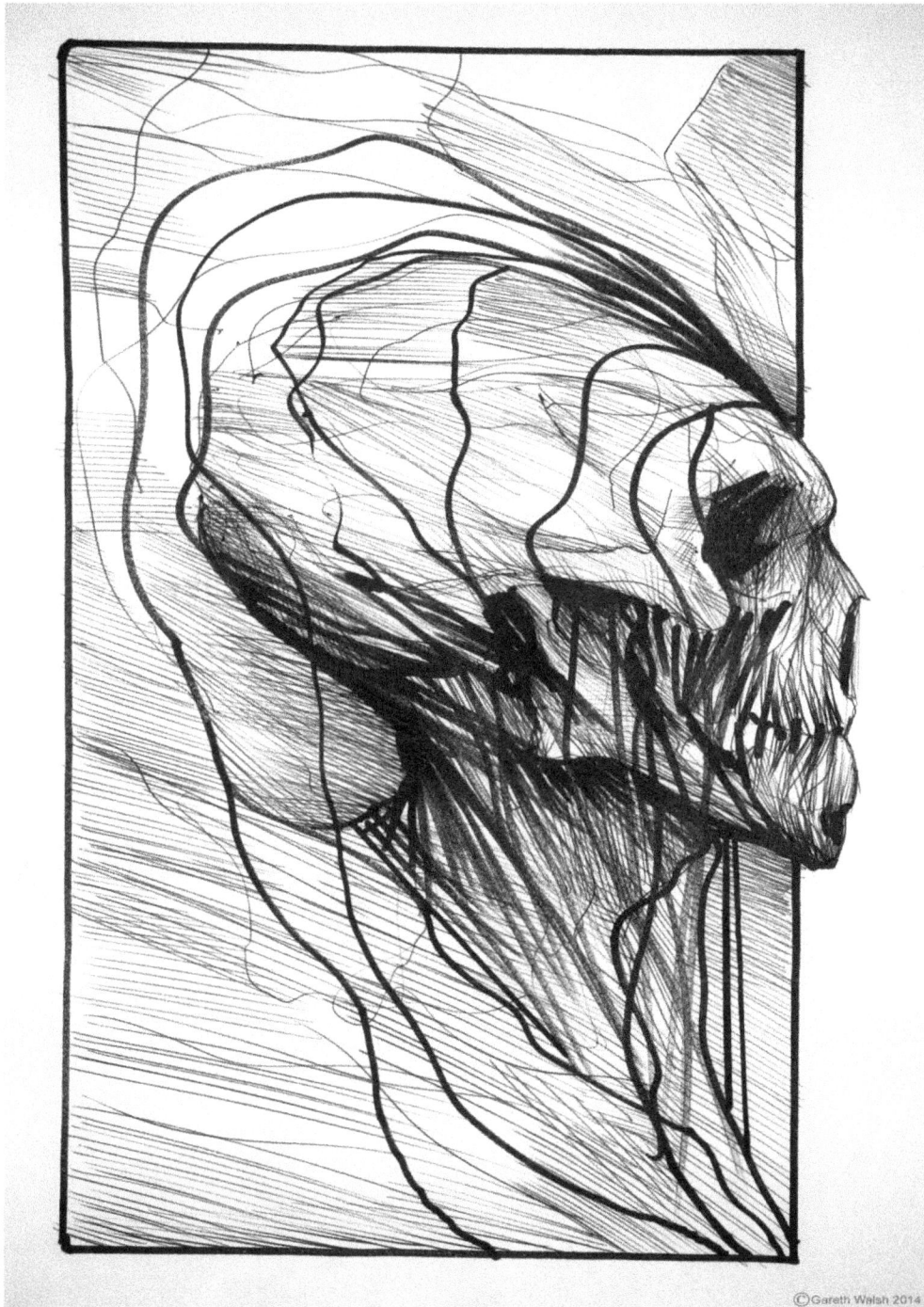

And it slipped out of grasp...silently faded into the past...blending into the thickening fog...like the faded memory of a forgotten song.

Once upon a time I was told I needed to be more sympathetic...empathetic...that I was on the road of a forgotten memory...an existential dead end...and the voice faded into the mists...further and further from where any light could penetrate the apathetic fog that had settled upon my soul...purgatorial punishment...limbo...delicately intertwined with the slowly slipping sands of time...but never alone...no never alone.

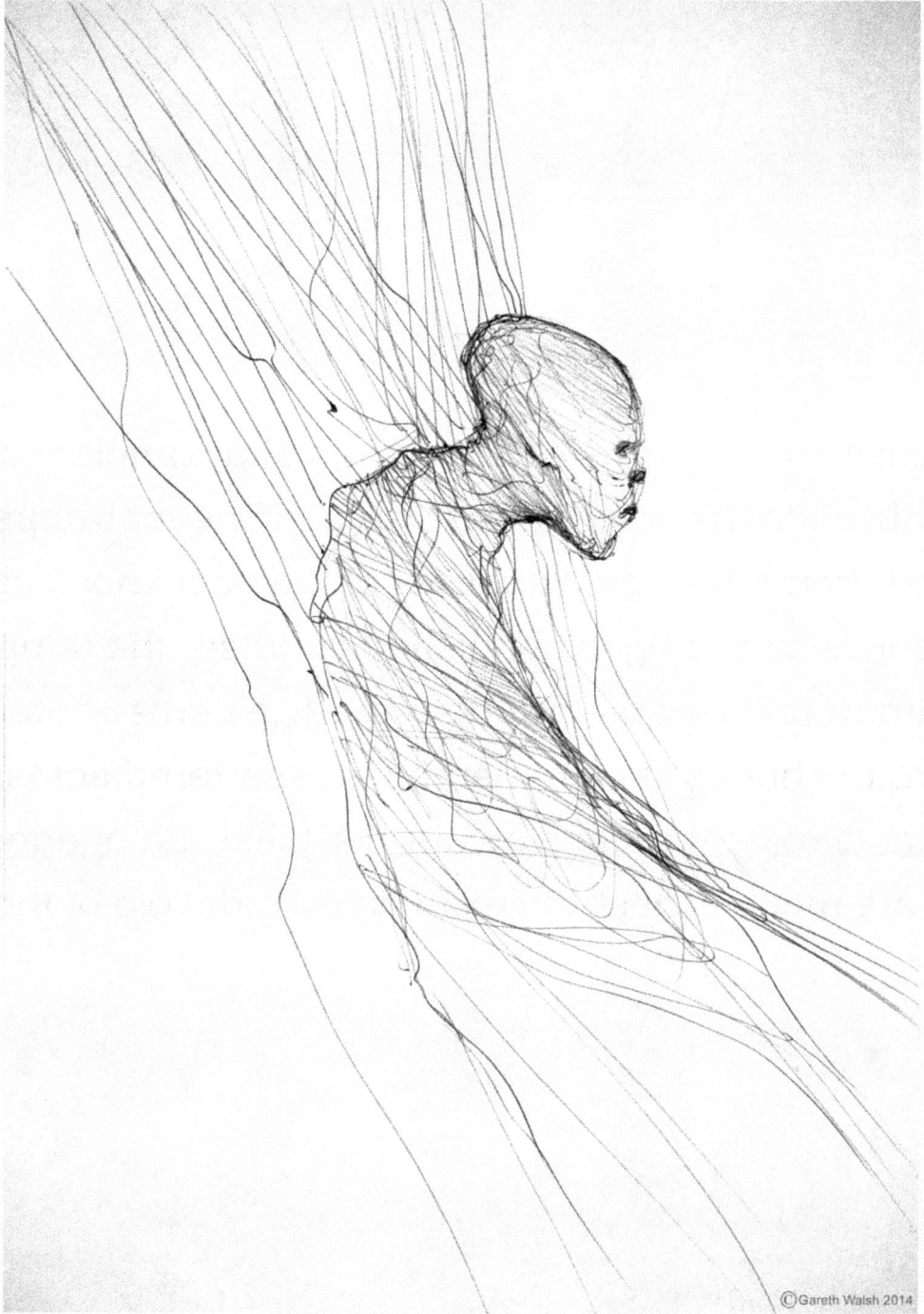

Incense smoke burns at a forgotten altar...ancient ones crumble into the void...vacant...a gaze forever trapped in stone...immortal...the witnesses of the past knock at the door...wax of long extinguished candles...the temple frozen...forever watching...onyx eyes...a crimson stained basin...the bones of past memories...scattered across the floor...an eloquent silence awaits the feast...an offering...the walls are made of flesh...blink of an eye...devoid of thought.

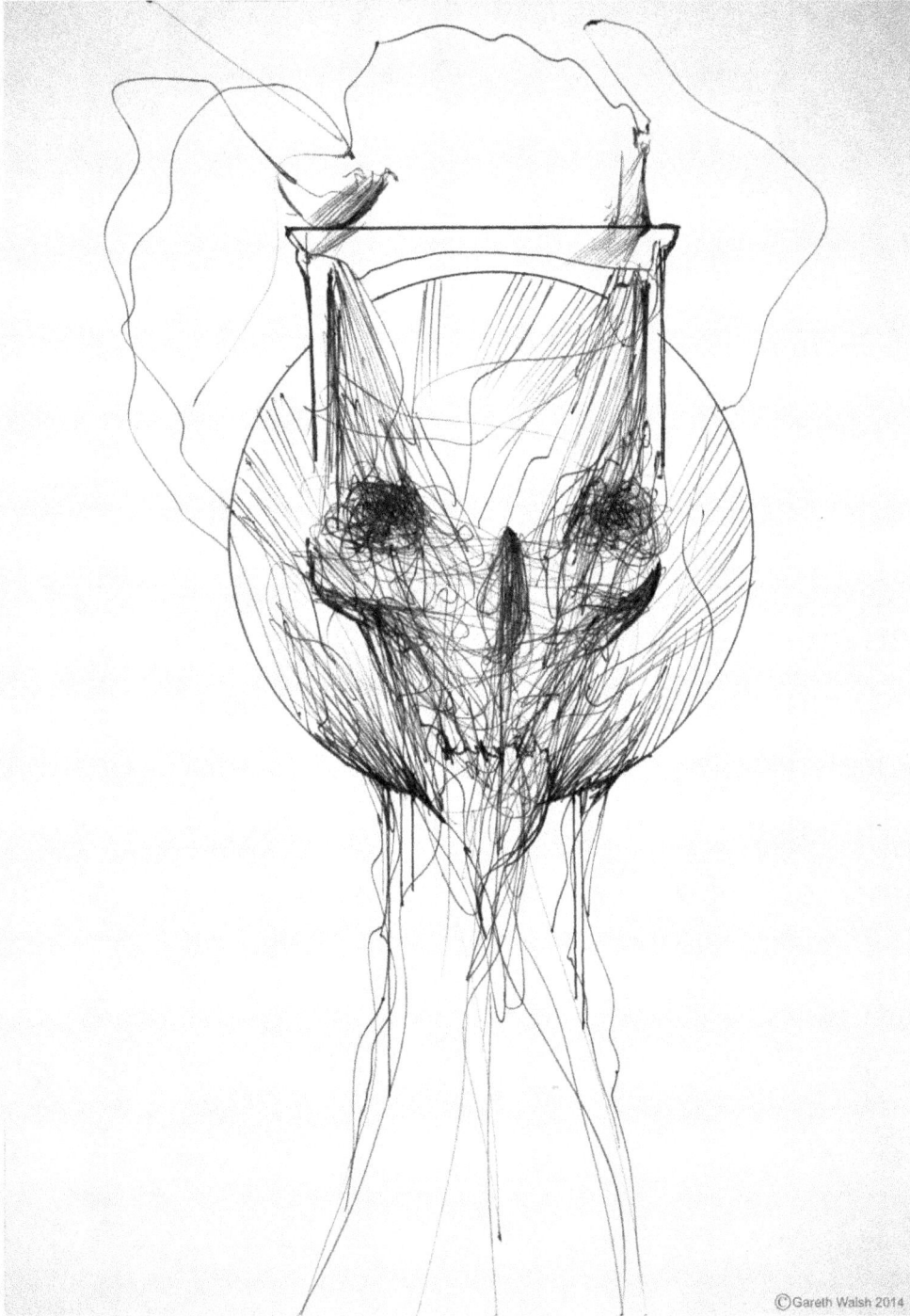

Aberrant vibrations...diluted revelations...the snake crawls across the desert floor...skin peel away...shedding layer upon layer...peel it back...follow the trail...towards the end...slithering...pull another layer back...enigmatic scriptures written on the arid floor...prophetic dreams in a seamless eternity...shed another layer...truth...absent meaning...crawl away...peel it back...venomous vibrations.

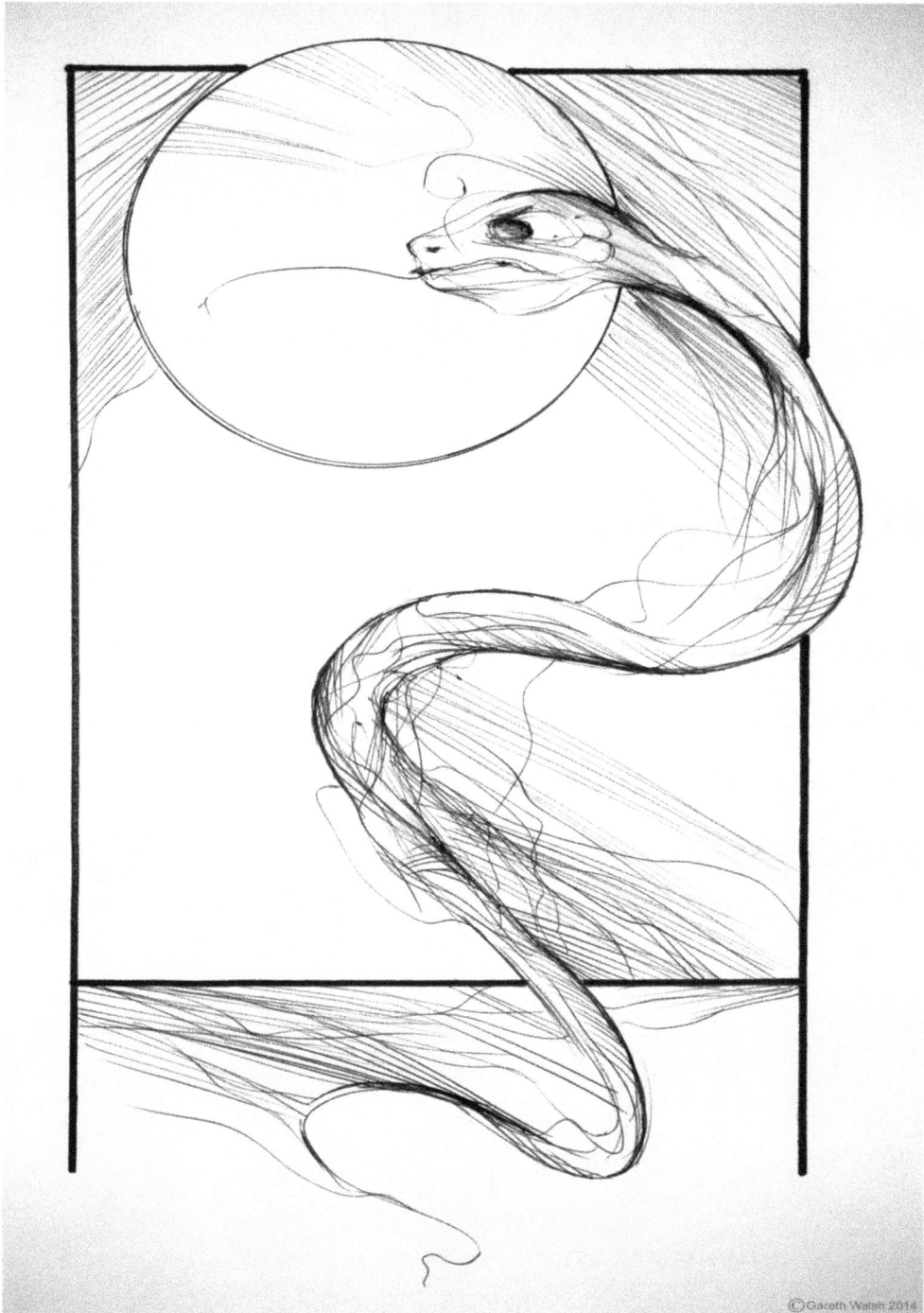

Cold black stillness...not a single light to the heavens above...a wayward stranger...a traveler...contemplative debates underneath an eons old abyss...the watchers stopped watching...aged...died away as the clock ticked...ancient memories all that remain...a solitary soul travels on...the abyss watches...quietly gazing down...waiting for it to drift away.

©Gareth Walsh 2014

A sweet melodic death...all consuming...festering...parasitic...repetition, repetition, repetition...plague, disease...never ceasing...noise...rage...hidden in dark corners...a trick of the angles...deceit, treachery...meaning found in solitude...scent of burning flesh and hair...tear it all away...forgotten...tossed into rotting catacombs...the dead speak...speak of forbidden knowledge...etheric realities beyond conscious thought...repetition, repetition, repetition...digging my own abode...one shovelful at a time...three by eight by six...one shovelful at a time...foreign tongues...skeletal fingers beckon...behind glass eyes...the space between...dreams in a broken shard...forever cold...my soul at auction...get the fuck out of here...insomniatic ranting as nightingales sing...this will all make sense...this will all (stop) making sense...seeking the light between cracked stones...repetition...finding meaning in the spaces between.

Dread...waking dreams...questions unanswered...shadows lurking...dark by design...a trail runs through the wall...hidden between remnants of past desires...step by step...walking back down this path...voices calling...beckoning...my own screams echo...resonating deep into my soul...and the ravens watch silently...always witness to the state of things...mockingly from the shadows...violins trail off in the distance...a sorrowful tune...blood on my hands...wipe away blinders...the yellow lines of the highway fly by...pure serenity...no feeling...flying away...same highway...same spiritual awakening...stillness...nothing but the sky...a touch of remorse on the breeze...in distant stars...the lights flicker...skeletal remnants of fantasies forgotten...deja vu...euphoric memories of childhoods past...menacing clouds on the horizon...the rabbits form a terrible procession...accusing stares among the cold throng...cold sweat...dark dreams of luciferian design...gasping for breath...night terrors...the trees bow their heads in disgrace...strangers at midnight...the gossip of the floorboards...their screams come from beneath...deafening...deafening...the yellow lines all fly by...monotonous...same song and dance...same story...the ink dries...the pages fade...the story unfinished.

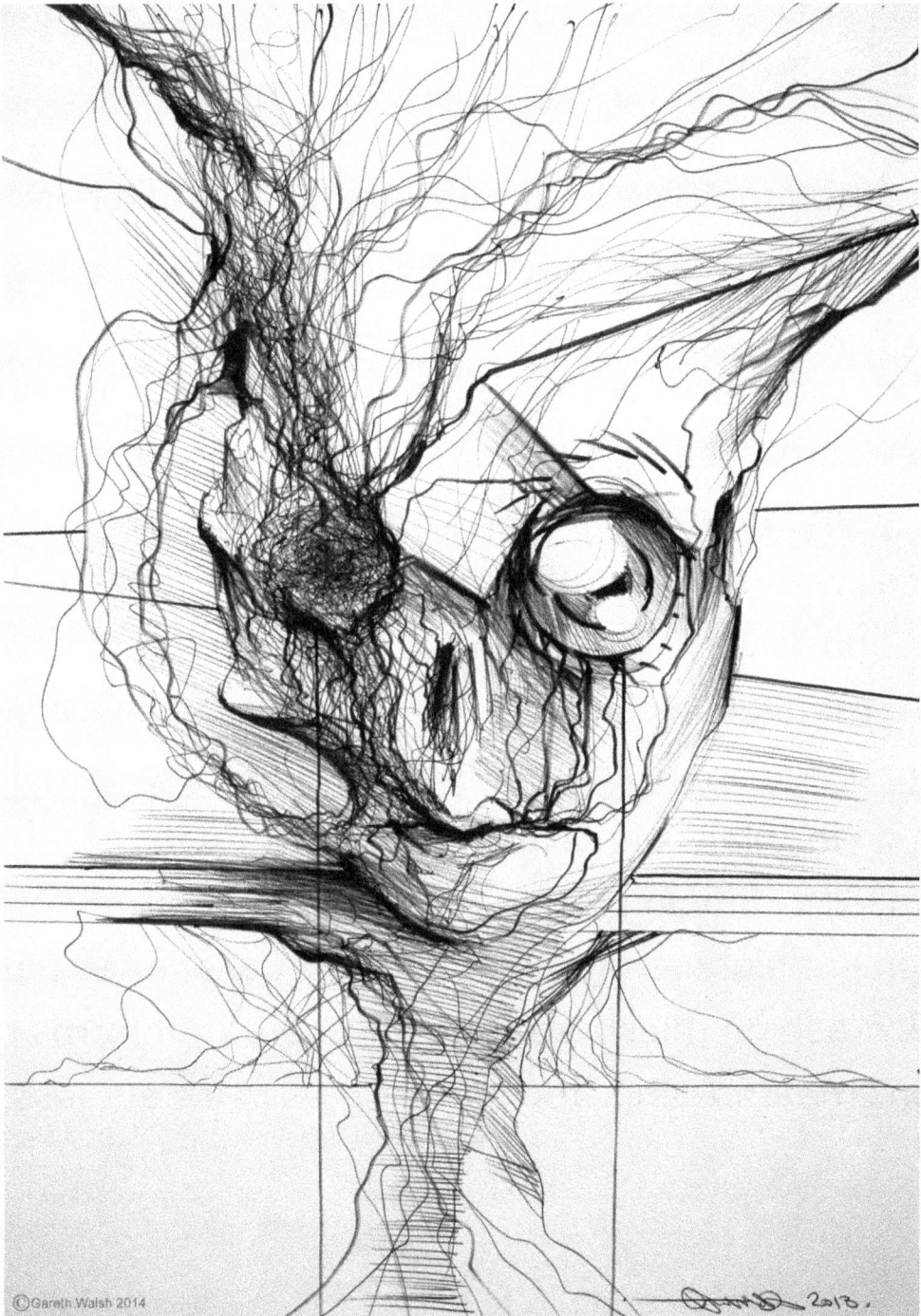

2013.

Broken thoughts...sunlight through half opened blinds...the dust slowly drifts down...settles...a lone voice is heard in the distance...pounding...listening to the heartbeat...controlled breathing...one, two, three...one, two, three...broken fragments of glass litter the floor...a cat wanders among the ghosts of the past...sixth sense...wandering aimlessly...pacing...the clock chimes obtrusively...broken thoughts...reaching deep within...meditative state...the water flows...waves crash on a darkened shore...nightfall...watching the waves flow in...black sand...the stones glisten in the moonlight...dancing round and round...creatures that go bump in the night...a tight knit circle, ritual of ages past...the waves crash on the shore...fine mist...thought forms on the horizon...materializing...the water flows in it's endless cycle.

Crumbling plaster...piece by piece cracking...veins extending out...blood splatter...a rorschach mask of crimson hues...enigmatic...choking...tightening grip...shattered skull...cold sweats...screams amongst secretions and torn flesh...blackening vision...the gateway of perdition gaping wide like the whore of Babylon...necessary pain...doll eyes, a silent witness...dozens of unblinking eyes...glimmering amongst the filth...chine white bone...echoes of reflected memories...the mirror shatters...the dolls smile...obscured revelations amongst the backdrop of a harlot's tears...necessary tears...moist lips...a narcissistic deity...no sign of heaven...no angels wept...destitute...the virgin amongst her dolls...filling the altar with tears shed in misery...lacerations adorn thy body...laughter from within...deep in the depths of a soul...the shadow creeps among discarded dreams and unredeemed love...the dust continues to fall...settling among discarded bodily fluids...dozens of eyes glitter as the lights go out.

©Gareth Walsh 2014

Eyes glint in the light of passing headlights...voyeuristic felines...the derelict stumbles and falls...alcohol impaired vision in the dirty alley...crouching...blending in with the shadows....the pack closes in...a sudden noise in the background...the cats run like rats, scattering...strike of a match...sulphur in the air...grinning smile looking down upon the disheveled man...extended hand, glass shimmering in the dimming light...addiction plagues the disease ridden body...parchment unfurled...forgotten names inscribed with blood...soul on a sleeve.

©Gareth Walsh 2014

Detachment on a summer breeze...the juries out, deceit...the judge's gavel comes down...deafening silence...the sentence yet to be proclaimed...the condemned hang in limbo...a purgatorial nightmare...contemplation...the circuitry long ago rotted away...tick tock...a broken heart, pierced by a dull blade...the razors worn but the blood fresh...up, up, up...a thin line between heaven and hell...unrequited desires among decaying flowers...funerary barge...floating out....sinking down...down into the murky waters of indecision...the gateway to bliss no where in sight...drowning...hands bound...no sight of a redeemer...no sign of any light from above...down into the murky waters.

Knocking along the walls...voices murmuring...I know what they say...can hear them clearly...auditory hallucinations...who is deceived among a world of illusions...thought creates and then destroys...nothing exists...all in my head...blink of an eye...is the world still here...universal suffering felt in millions of consciousness's...fear ingrained in our psyche...created by the same vision...do not be fooled by the eyes.

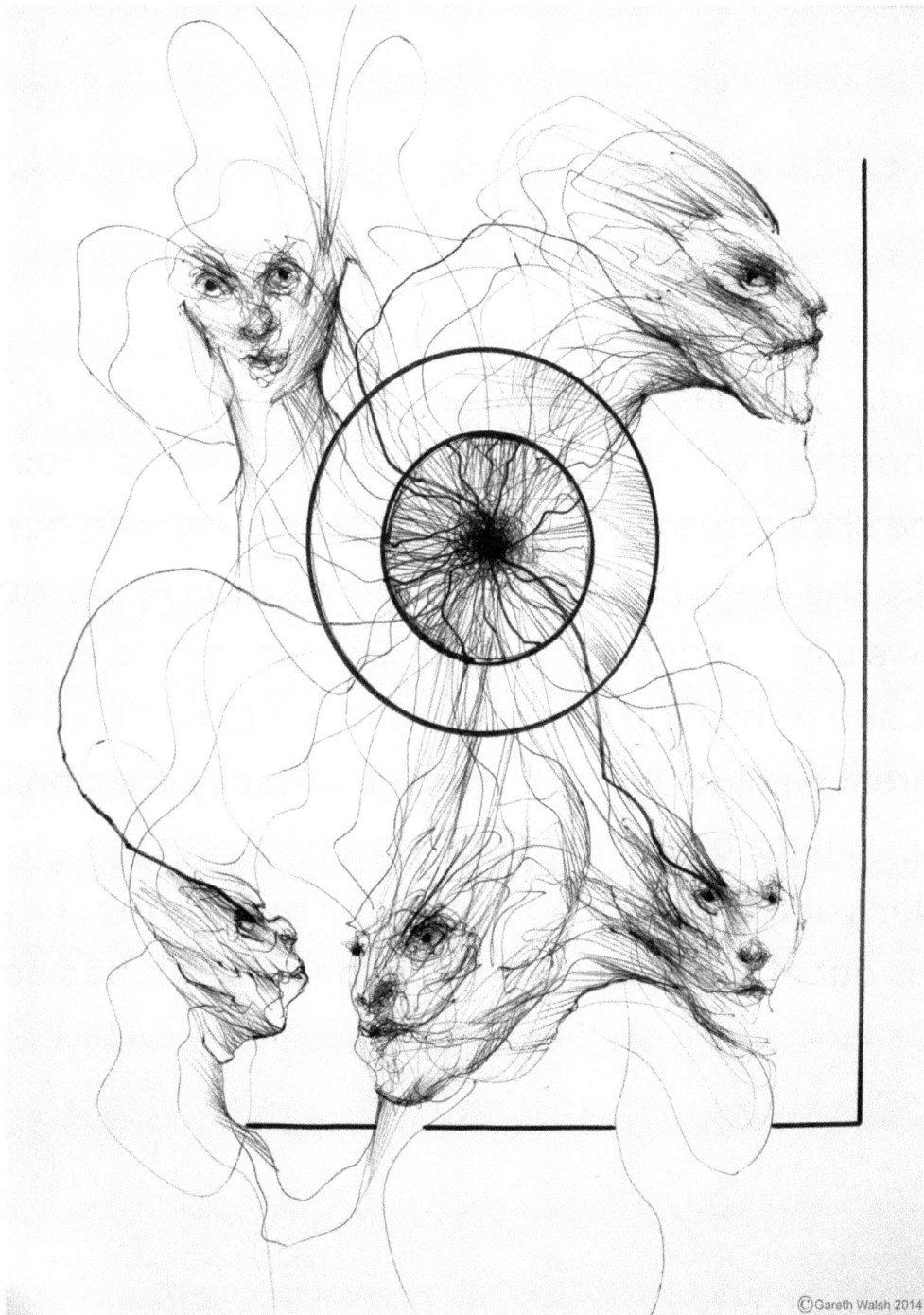

©Gareth Walsh 2014

First sight...deepest greens transform to shades of fire...the cold northern winds sweep down as the plants expire...as the sky turns subtle shades of grey the green man rests...the sounds of the world die away and the world grows silent...encased with ice...committed to a frozen tomb...the remaining drift by in slow motion...Skadi wraps the forest within her white blanket...Hades ceremoniously flings opens the doors...gateways to the underworld...welcoming souls with open arms...rebirth seems out of reach...the long season of death has begun.

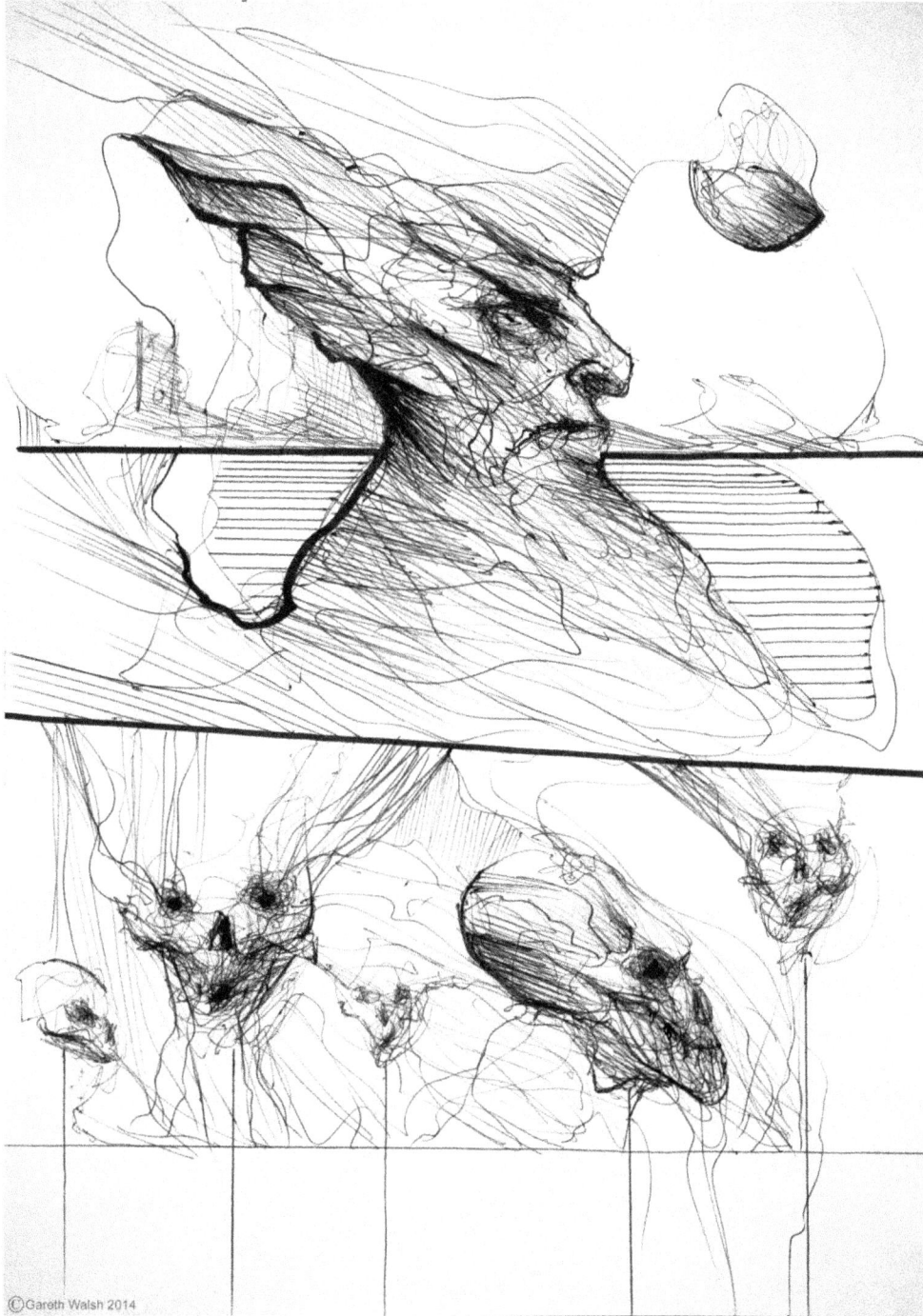

Gasping for breath...night terrors awake me...scent of incense clings to the air...shadows cling to the corners of the moonlit room as faded glimpses of hellish dreams flash in my memory...moonlight streams in from an open window and it's as if the night air is choking...stumbled out of bed...sinister noises surround me...loss of direction...for a moment the world seems upside down...the rusted pipes creak and groan under the weight of the decaying house...in moments of contemplation I find myself in the basement...cold stone and spiders my confessors...they hear my sins without judgment...water drips somewhere in the distance...darkness...footfalls somewhere overhead...strike of a match...the candle putters to life, it's wick dancing with a cool breeze from an unknown source...scent of sulphur...demons in the air...flickering...sitting alone...my confessions a tale spun in the web of the spiders that are always listening.

©Gareth Walsh 2014

Unearthly silence...a melancholy soliloquy under a Stygian firmament...Luna reduced to a solitary sliver in the sky...starless...gazing up into the void...an abysmal feeling of dread settles in as foreboding clouds eclipse her...bittersweet tinged flashes above...the trees illuminated...skeletal frames reaching out...necrophagous shadows roam the ravaged landscape as I sit perched and pondering beneath the violet illumination...flashes...they creep closer as Luna disappears beneath an asphyxiating blanket...and oddly enough this dance has a serene quality...this dance of death...as the shadows tear the limbs from anything unlucky enough to be revealed...cracking bones and torn flesh...a necrotic paradise beneath the ever threatening presence of the abyss...traveling down the river Styx...searching...seeking Eurydice amongst forgotten memories and discarded dreams...the gondolier's face is shrouded...the water an onyx hue...no sign of heaven in sight.

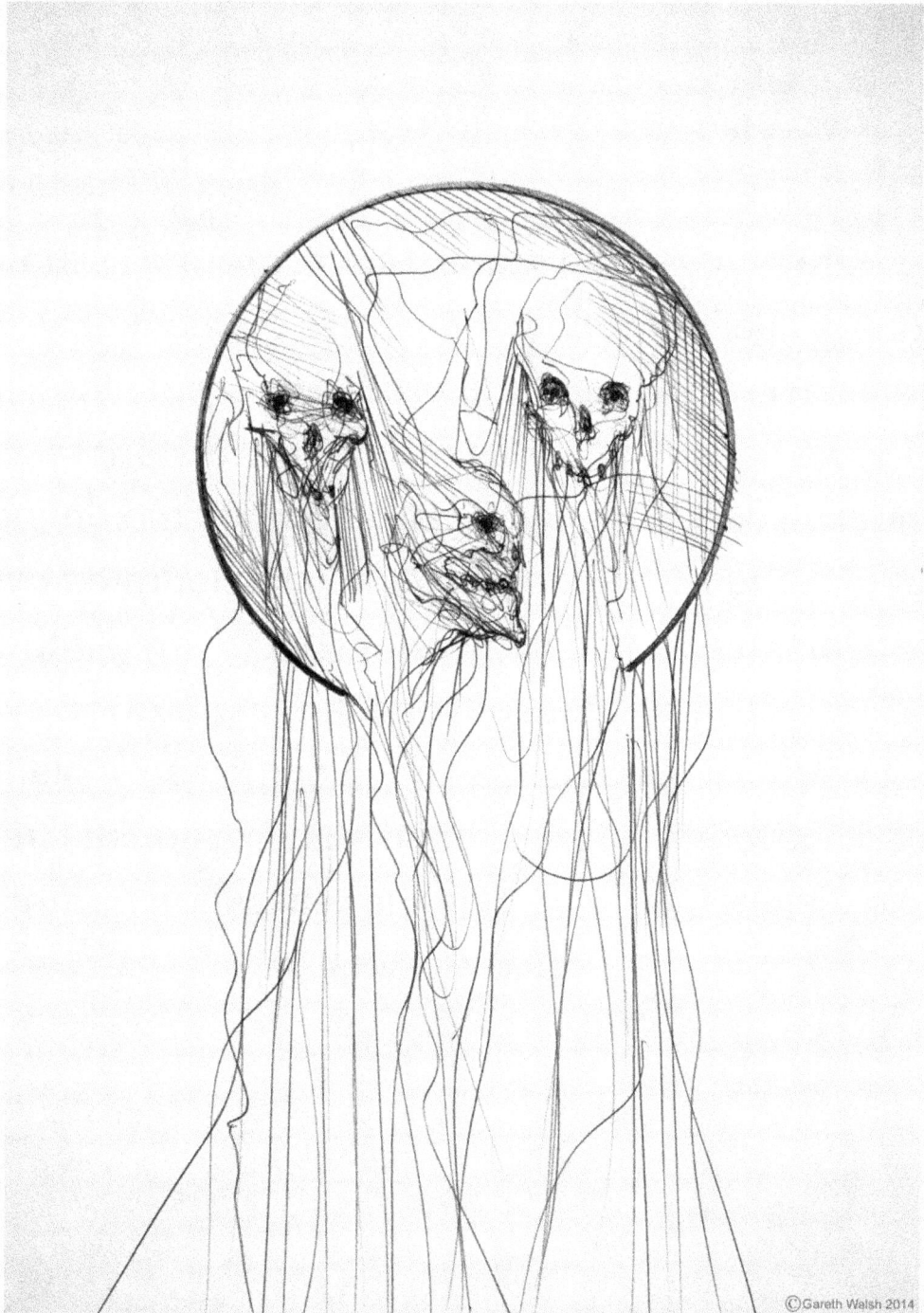

The rain drops painted pictures on the ground...silhouettes of bedtime fleetingly glimpsed across the backdrop of the night...crickets chirped and predators crept along like shadows between flashes of light and distant rolls of thunder...a dark path lay ahead...beneath the ominous blanket of clouds that blotted out the sky...looming over the spiraling landscape...a dark shadow had been glimpsed by the third eye...ever present yet changing around every bend...it was as if a tear in the fabric of the astral plane had been discovered...all time stood still...frozen...still frame within a distant memory...then the realization hit...the way out is within.

An icy touch...cold breath...fire falls from the sky...drifting...slowly falling upon the ground..the landscape barren, skeletal remains of the garden of Eden...a lone raven watches from a distant perch...carrion comfort, as Boreas sweeps the land...the sun is eclipsed as cryptid nightmares awake...barricaded indoors mortal life seems fleeting...prey to the unknown that roam the darkness...a single flame to hold back obscure visions...gone in a wisp of smoke.

From aggregate shards the word is formed...heretical apostasy...the king barricaded in his city of ivory...false idols...from the throne room the crimson tide worships...wave after wave...poisoning from the pulpit...leading the lambs to the slaughter...no messiah...no purgatory...an aged hermit dangles by one foot...the fool gazes up at the star for divine intervention...the Earth trembles and the winds blow...the message lost...buried beneath shrouds of decadence and tongue of contradictions...diseased, the emperor struggles for breath...before him a kingdom of sulphur...vain struggles...death rattle...gasping for breath...the house of Thelema arises from the dust...fais ce que tu veux.

Somber skies ominously loom...visions of past remembrance...a cool breeze sweeps the expanse carrying the sounds of the night...yawning from forgotten caves...the heavens are within a finger's grasp...solitary meditation...smoke curls...twisting and winding out into the shadows...watching...a whispered breath lost in a moment...the light dims as everything fades to black...in the air a forgotten dream...just out of reach...crawling back to the beginning...carried away by the breeze.

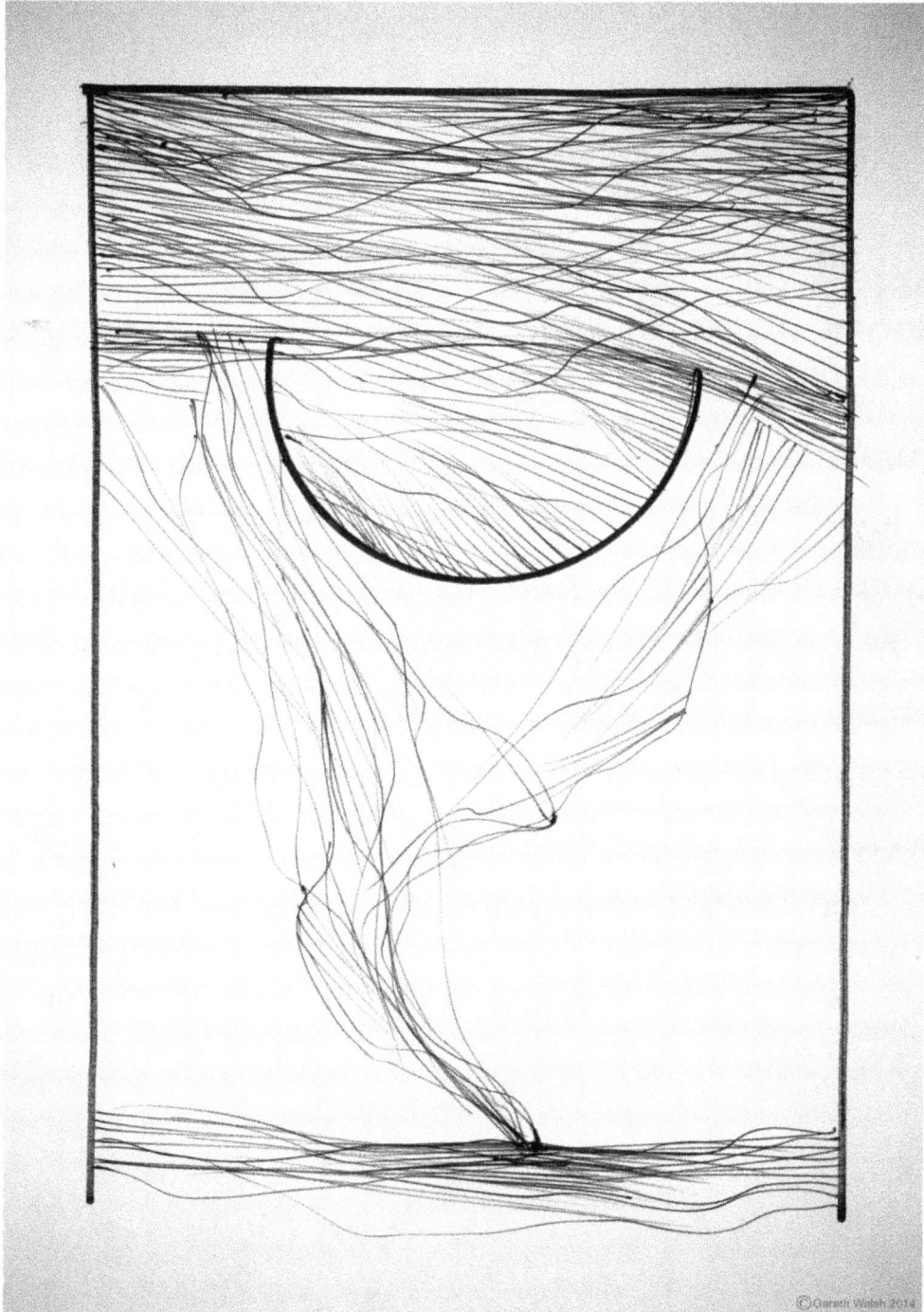

Hunger...a state of mind...ritualistic fasting before the slaughter...feverish haze...time slows to a crawl...the crack in the wall deepens...sudden calmness...serenity...I blink my eyes as sweat drips down...one second...two seconds...time consumed...the lotus petals open one by one upon the pedestal...crown chakra...third eye wide...blink...into the etheric realm...astral flight...one by one the petals fall to the path ahead...stepping stones guiding the way...bringing me home...bringing peace...step by step...a solitary moment in the fabric of time.

The crone rambles...incessant noise...debris scattered across wastelands of once fertile Earth...aged, the once smooth skin folds and creases...and not a thought is given in regards to her well being...spittle flies from cracked lips...a cacophony issues forth like a savage flock of birds...death stands at the door knocking...bony fingers grip the knob...opening, a mirror is revealed...reflected images...the crone stares into her own eyes...no recognition...the cold hands of death lift her into the breeze...an instant of terror...flung to the winds...dust to dust.

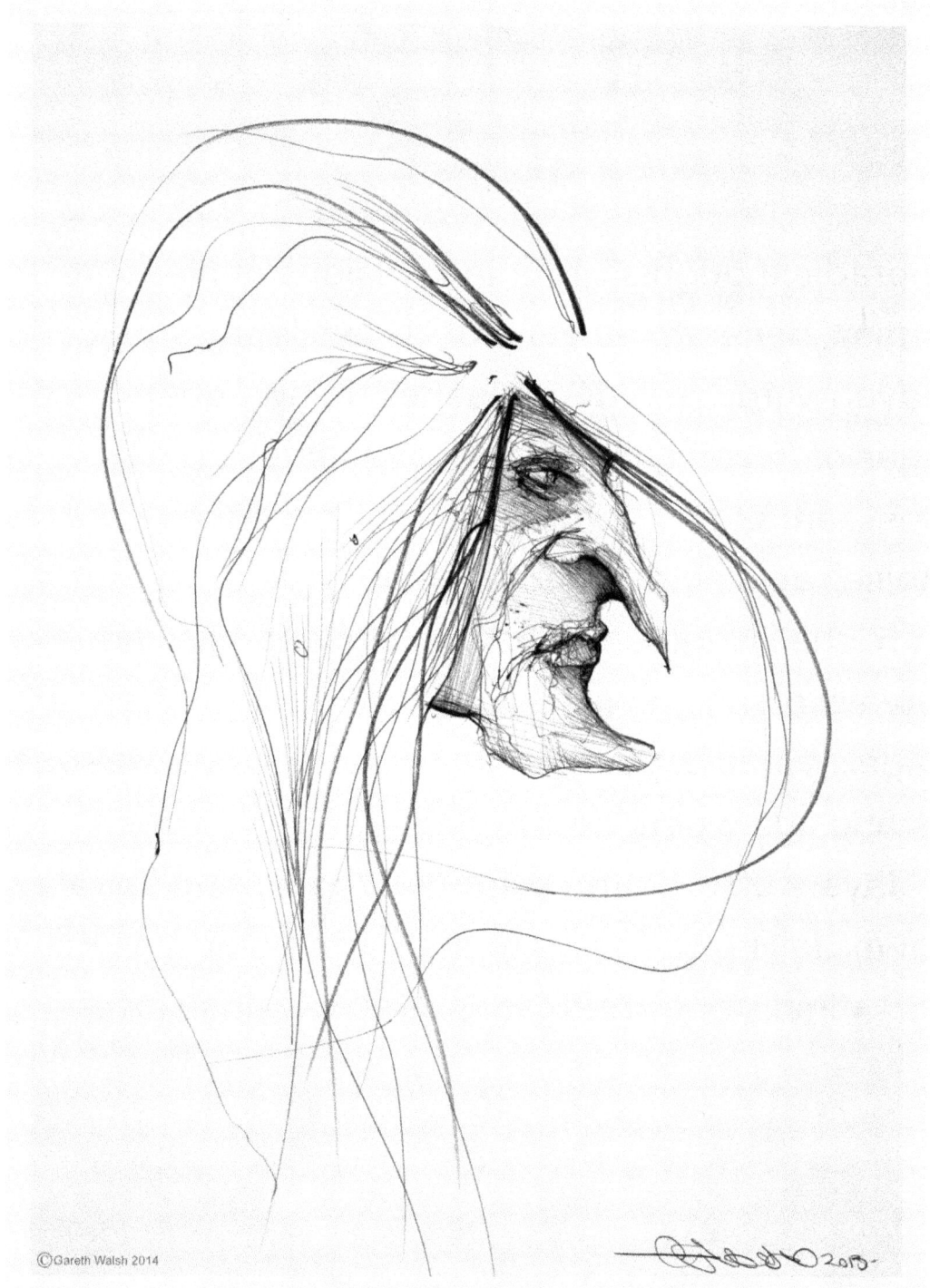

Sporadic thoughts...jumbled illusions of pleasure and disdain...beneath the glow of Luna silently smoke drifts heavenward...smoldering ashes below...deep beneath ages of frozen time...a lone raven cries out, it's voice lost...entangled beneath so much feedback...white noise...an electric hum in the air...true art is found in death...the living tread threw thickening bile...not even a sideways glance towards the starving sage...derelict and savage...words of poetry and prose pour out...drowned in this static age where beauty is dead...buried deep beneath layers of forgotten symbols...the writing spirals down...falling...dripping to the Earth below...as the ink finally dries and fades...the curtains close.

The minutes tick by...confessions bleed threw torn pages...chimes in a distant hall...midnight...sleepless nights and regretted recollections...discarded memories crumpled on the floor...listless...dreams intertwine with waking thoughts...tangled up in astral webs...etheric spiders weave a tale...behind closed eyes...shut but all seeing...blink...tick tock...into the depths...down into the darkness...past the gates...threw the hidden angles...beyond the darkened city.

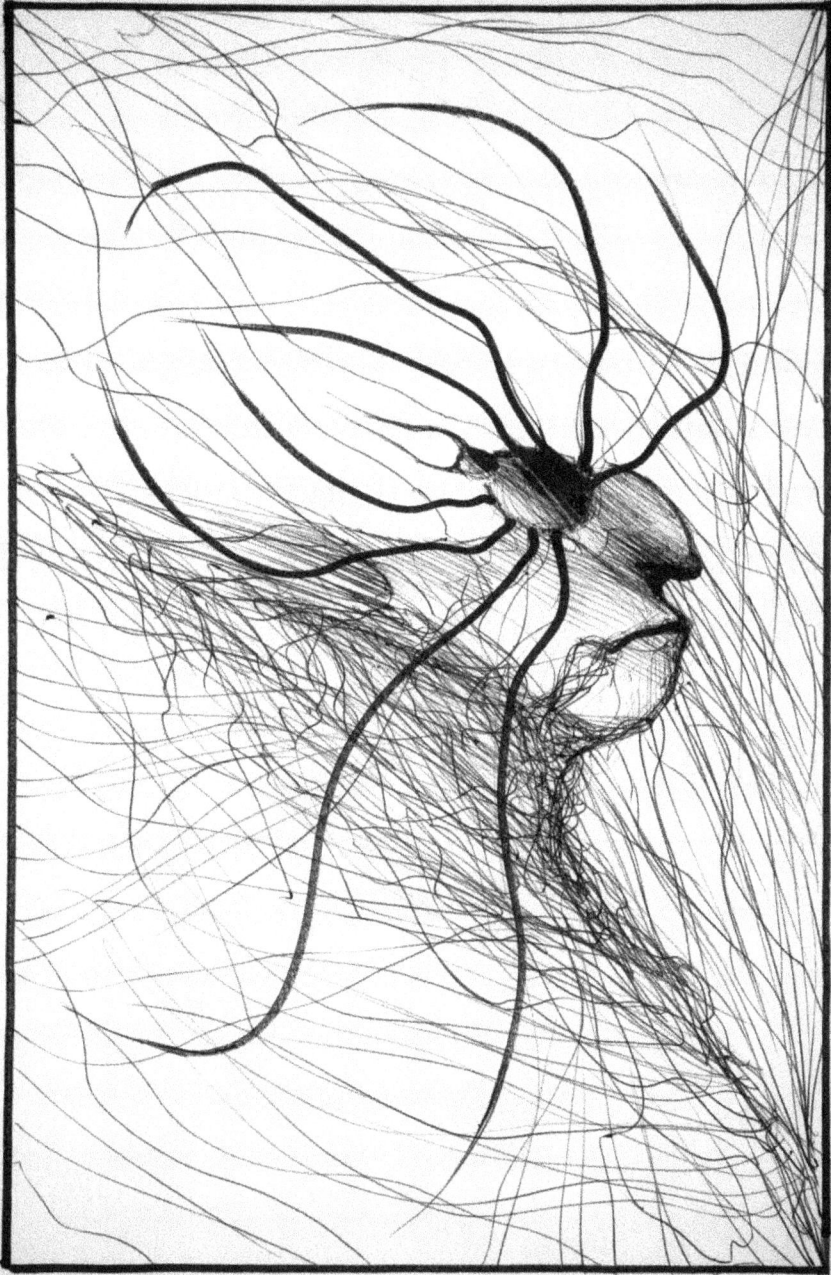

Beyond the veil of mist...peering threw keyholes I seek the truth in the spaces between...down beneath cracked and aging wood...cryptic answers below layers of dust...a faint glimpse of light...aura...phantoms peer curiously from the corners...old superstitions and memories that hide between sight...forgotten muscle memory...transcending the program...astral walk...hidden in the angles...evaporating into the beyond...crossing the thirteen gates.

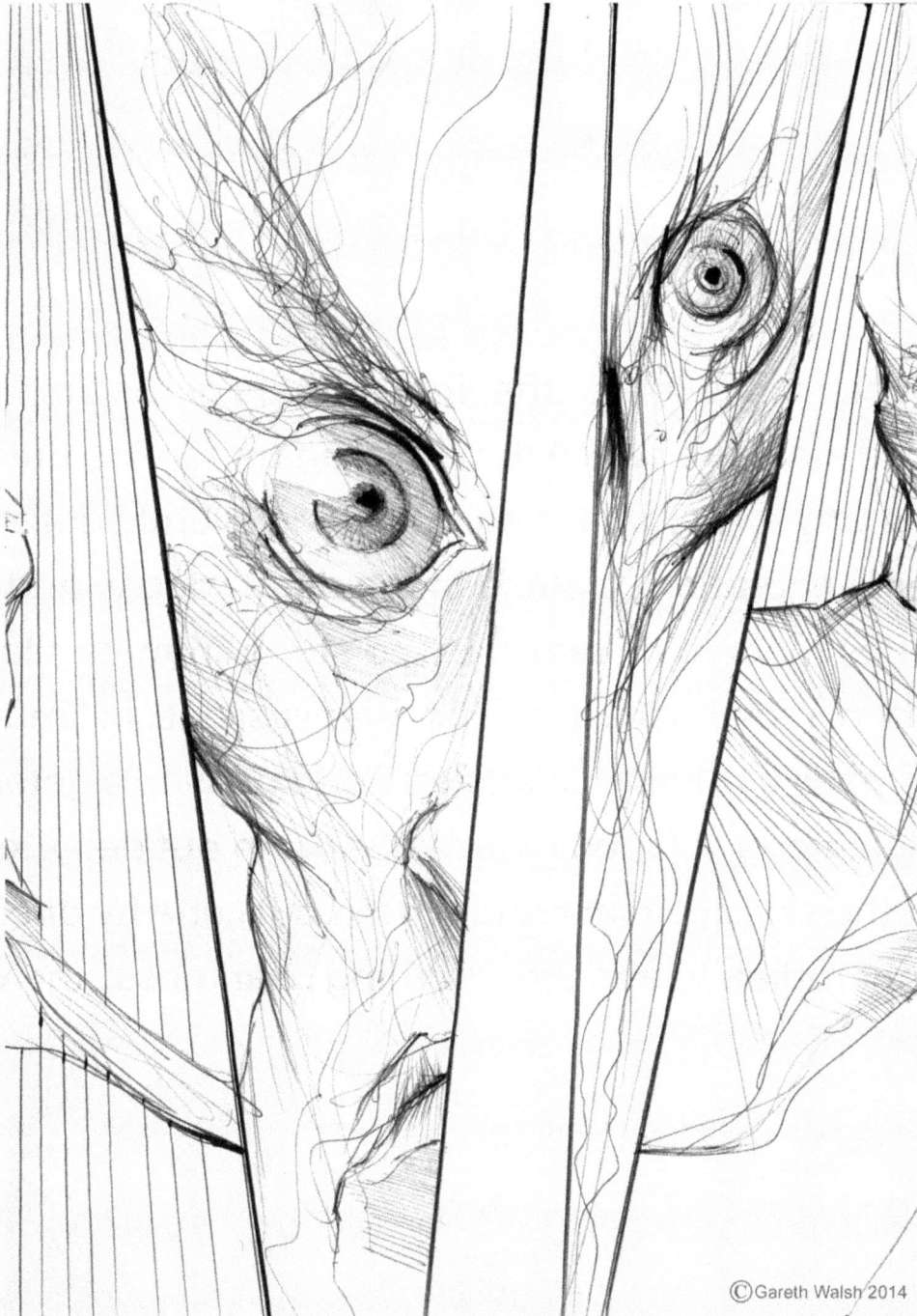

A silent calm...darkness...the final embers of the fire fade as scattered stars are all the remains...an unnerving quiet...the ceremony has ended...patches of fog silently drift over rotting vegetation...a place of the dead...decay and lost reveries marked by rain washed stone...names silently forgotten, reclaimed...the bell tower is silent...in limbo the spirits pass by...hell is a fairy tale and heaven's gates are shut...left alone, a faded dream of a worn out deity...clouds dot the sky...the stars are blotted out...one by one...a brilliant radiance and then nothing...darkness...the void.

Painted within shattered dreams...stained shards of a broken heart...the cold grip of loneliness...uncertainty...traveling along a forgotten trail...untended, nature threatens to reclaim...tangled in briars and weeds...frozen fingers reach from the depths...beckoning towards a downward spiral...as a prayer issues forth from frostbitten lips...a wish on a fallen star...grasping to the remembrance of warmth that once consumed this soul...looking for the north star to guide the way...past the barriers...trials and tribulations await at every turn...into the darkness of the shadow...yet hope remains.

©Gareth Walsh 2014

"To see nothing is to perceive the Way, and to understand nothing is to know the Dharma, because seeing is neither seeing nor not seeing and because understanding is neither understanding nor not understanding."
-Bodhidharma